URSA

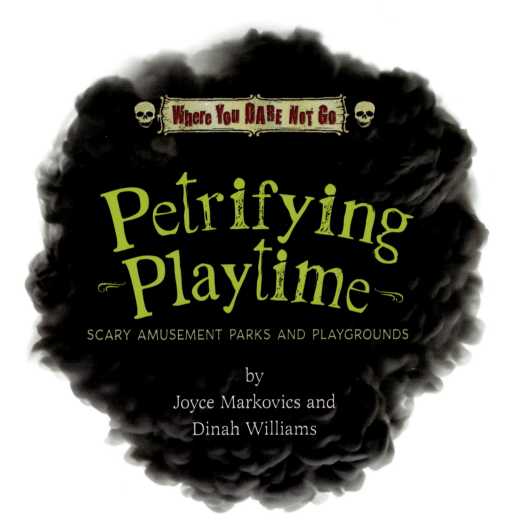

Where You DARE Not Go

Petrifying Playtime

SCARY AMUSEMENT PARKS AND PLAYGROUNDS

by
Joyce Markovics and
Dinah Williams

BEARPORT
PUBLISHING

Minneapolis, Minnesota

Credits

Cover, © rgc1983/Shutterstock, © Dean Drobot/Shutterstock, © MarlonTravel/Shutterstock, © CapturePB/Shutterstock, and © Daniela Pelazza/Shutterstock; 4–5, © Valeriy Matveyev/iStock, © BrAt_PiKaChU/iStock, © Little River/Shutterstock, © Picture-Syndicate/Shutterstock, © FOTOKITA/ iStock, and © Emukuf/Dreamstime.com; 6, © Chronicle/Alamy Stock Photo; 7, © Public Domain/Wikimedia Commons and © Douglas County Historical Society of Omaha, Nebraska; 8, © Billy McDonald/Adobe Stock; 9, © modify260/Adobe Stock, © Uladzimir/Adobe Stock, and © serikbaib/Adobe Stock; 10, © Pacific Ocean Park/Wikimedia Commons; 11, © Pacific Ocean Park/wikimedia Commons; 12, © Eduardo Carneglia/Flickr; 14, © Belikova Oksana/Adobe Stock; 16, © Blueflutterflies/Dreamstime.com; 17, © Elnur/ Adobe Stock, © Lustre/Adobe Stock, © Kamenetskiy Konstantin/Shutterstock, and © Roman Samborskyi/ Shutterstock; 18, © Edd Lange/Shutterstock; 19, © Edward/Adobe Stock and , © lotosfoto/Adobe Stock; 20, © Smallbones/Creative Commons CC0 1.0 Universal Public Domain Dedication; 21, © N-gio/ Creative Commons Attribution-Share Alike 4.0 International; 22, © Boone County Sheriff's Office; 23, © John McDonald; 24, © Ritu Manoj Jethani/Shutterstock; 25, © Ritu Manoj Jethani/Shutterstock; 26, © Missouri Valley Special Collections, Kansas City Public Library; 27, © Mikhail Bakunovich/Shutterstock; 28, © UPI/ Alamy Stock Photo; 29, © Kristina Rogers/Shutterstock; 30, © Brian/Adobe Stock; 31, © Hulton Archive /Getty Images; 32, © Niagara Falls (Ontario) Public Library; 34, © Yuval Helfman/Adobe Stock; 35, © carlatayler/Shutterstock; 36, © Kemter/iStock; 37, © JoelMasson/Adobe Stock; 38, © Lysha R. Stanford/ Flickr; 39, © LonelyPilgrim/Creative Commons Attribution 2.5 Generic; 40, © Colourpicture/Wikimedia Commons; 41, © Thomas Byrne/Creative Commons Attribution-Share Alike 3.0 Unported.

Bearport Publishing Company Product Development Team

President: Jen Jenson; Director of Product Development: Spencer Brinker; Managing Editor: Allison Juda; Associate Editor: Naomi Reich; Associate Editor: Tiana Tran; Art Director: Colin O'Dea; Designer: Kim Jones; Designer: Kayla Eggert; Product Development Assistant: Owen Hamlin

Statement on Usage of Generative Artificial Intelligence

Bearport Publishing remains committed to publishing high-quality nonfiction books. Therefore, we restrict the use of generative AI to ensure accuracy of all text and visual components pertaining to a book's subject. See BearportPublishing.com for details.

Library of Congress Cataloging-in-Publication Data is available at www.loc.gov or upon request from the publisher.

ISBN: 979-8-89232-075-7 (hardcover)
ISBN: 979-8-89232-607-0 (paperback)
ISBN: 979-8-89232-208-9 (ebook)

For more information, write to Bearport Publishing, 5357 Penn Avenue South, Minneapolis, MN 55419.

Contents

Play at Your Own Risk

Everyone needs somewhere to play. But what happens when a place that used to bring so much joy turns more frightening than fun? A swing slowly begins to sway back and forth in an empty playground, and the patter of small feet sound across the grass. But when you look around, you see nothing. Has a spirit come out to play?

An eerie scream fills the silence in the abandoned amusement park. Nothing is around to make the fear-filled sound . . . or to hear it. What led to the tragic ends to places that once brought so much happiness? And what has stayed behind?

The Crash of the Coaster

Krug Park introduced a number of new attractions in 1913. They included an airplane ride, a penny arcade, and a huge merry-go-round that had 72 horses. The most exciting attraction of all, however, was the Big Dipper roller coaster.

Krug Park

By 1930, the Big Dipper roller coaster in Krug Park had made riders scream for 17 years. That summer, however, the joyful shrieks turned to cries of pain. On July 24, just after 6:00 p.m., a bolt on the wooden coaster came loose, causing four cars to crash through a rotten guardrail. Twenty-three riders plunged 30 feet (9 m) to the ground. The cars landed on top of them, killing 4 and injuring 17 others.

The terrible accident marked the beginning of the end for Krug Park. Soon after the crash, government leaders in Omaha banned amusement parks in the city from running roller coasters. As a result, Krug Park lost business each year until it closed in 1940. It stood eerily empty for the next 15 years.

The Big Dipper after the accident

Police arrive on the scene

In 1955, Krug Park was turned into a city park with baseball fields, a playground, and a swimming pool. The once-abandoned amusement park also got a new name: Gallagher Park.

Haunted Hawaii

This small park is tucked away under a grove of tall trees on the volcanic Big Island of Hawaii. Hardened black lava covers the ground like a death shroud. What unearthly creatures roam around the area?

MacKenzie State Park

In the 1800s, prisoners were forced to work in the park. Swinging pickaxes, they carved out trails in the hard ground. Long after they died, their ghosts are said to still wander the grounds. The shadowy figures appear unshaven and half starved, dragging tools behind them.

According to reports, campers in the park have been awakened by bloodcurdling screams. Sometimes, an unseen force unzips their sleeping bags. "That place—I really believe—is haunted," said one visitor. "I just got goosebumps thinking about it."

In addition to the ghosts of dead prisoners, native Hawaiians believe the park is home to night marchers. These spirits of long-dead Hawaiians supposedly walk along the trails during the night. They grasp ghostly torches and pound drums. If you see them, locals say you should drop to the ground and stay very still. That's the only way the spirits will spare your life.

On the blackest nights, the spirit of a former prisoner called Louie is said to appear to visitors. It's believed that he killed another inmate and later died in the park.

Scorched Dreams

In 1957, amusement park designers spent $10 million creating a seaside wonderland in Santa Monica, California. When Pacific Ocean Park (POP) opened in 1958, its owners hoped it would be as popular as nearby Disneyland. Less than 20 years later, however, the pier was far from magical. It was a pile of smoking rubble.

Pacific Ocean Park

For just 90 cents, visitors to the newly opened POP could enjoy many different attractions. They included King Neptune's Courtyard, the Sea Circus, and the Westinghouse Enchanted Forest exhibit. The 28-acre (11-ha) park on the pier also featured the Sea Serpent roller coaster and the Ocean Skyway, a gondola that took people on a half-mile (0.8 km) trip out to sea.

Even with great rides, POP had trouble attracting customers. The pier was in a part of town where families didn't feel safe. By 1965, the park had started to look run-down and was getting fewer and fewer visitors. In October 1967 it closed for good.

Soon after, someone began setting fires on the pier. The first was in December 1969. Six months later, an even larger fire broke out at midnight. Thousands watched as the pier's ballroom went up in flames. More fires over the next several years slowly destroyed a park that once had more than 1,000,000 visitors a year. After a final blaze in 1974, the pilings that had once held up the pier were all that remained of POP.

In the 1970s, a group of daredevil teenagers from Santa Monica, nicknamed the Z-Boys, surfed among the ruins of POP. They later became famous for both surfing and skateboarding.

The Ocean Skyway gondola

A Spooky Swing

At first glance, Firmat, Argentina, looks like any other small city. However, there's a petrifying playground that has the whole city spooked.

The spooky playground in Firmat, Argentina

In June 2007, residents noticed something strange at a local playground. A swing began moving back and forth. Yet nobody was on it. The people wondered whether it was being pushed by the wind. Then, for 10 days in a row, the swing kept moving on its own—even on windless days. *Creak-creak. Creak-creak. Creak-creak.*

Concerned locals asked the police to investigate. After examining the swing, the officers had no idea what was causing it to move on its own. They found no strings tied to the swing or anything else unusual about it. Even when the police stopped the swing from moving, it quickly picked up momentum again.

All the while, teachers, parents, and children had their own explanation. "We believe it's haunted," said Maria de Silva Agustina, a local teacher. According to one legend, a child was accidentally killed on a construction site not far from where the swing set was built. Could this explain why the spooky swing would never stop . . . or was it really just the wind? The question remains. ∽⟫⟩

The police in Firmat contacted a team of scientists to uncover the mystery. They were stumped as well.

Nuclear Ghost Town

PRIPYAT AMUSEMENT PARK
PRIPYAT, UKRAINE

The new amusement park in Pripyat was supposed to open on May 1, 1986. To the surprise of the people in town, however, the park opened early on April 27. For a few hours, visitors enjoyed the Ferris wheel, the bumper cars, and other rides. Yet the very next day, the park was closed . . . never to open again.

Pripyat after it was abandoned

Why did a brand-new amusement park have such a short history? The park was built less than 2 miles (3 km) away from the Chernobyl nuclear power plant. An explosion at the plant on April 26, 1986, destroyed one of its reactors, sending clouds of poisonous smoke into the air.

Most of the people who lived in Pripyat worked at Chernobyl. At first, no one was sure how dangerous the situation was. The government didn't want anyone to panic, so those in charge opened the amusement park ahead of schedule to keep people calm. However, the scope of the danger soon became clear. The amount of radiation in the air was enough to kill a person. Several people living in Pripyat became sick right away. The town was evacuated.

At first, people were told they could expect to be back in a few days. But years later, the town of Pripyat and its amusement park remain empty. The radiation levels are still too dangerous for humans to live there. Wolves and deer now roam the once-bustling city. And the Ferris wheel still sits, silently waiting for riders to climb aboard.

Today, visitors can take a short tour of Pripyat. They go there to see a town frozen in time, filled with the toys, books, and other belongings that people left behind.

Watch Your Step!

Hummel Park stretches across hundreds of spooky, wooded acres. Stone steps lead to quiet walking trails. The park may look picture-perfect. But it holds horrible secrets.

The Morphing Stairs at Hummel Park

Hummel Park is said to be one of the spookiest spots in Nebraska. Some people say the park's mysterious stone staircase is cursed. Called the Morphing Stairs, visitors claim that the number of steps changes, depending on whether a person is walking up the stairs or down them.

Other visitors have sworn they've seen strange-looking people with bright white hair wandering around the park at night. Still others mention a hermit who lives in a tiny house in the woods. It's said that he'll make a meal out of anything that breathes!

In addition to these dark legends, terrible things have actually happened in the park. Between 1933 and 2006, three people were found dead there.

Is the park haunted? "Go out there at midnight and see how uneasy you feel," says a man who lives near the park. "You'll hear noises you don't normally think possible."

In 1930, a wealthy family donated 200 acres (80 ha) of land to the city of Omaha. The area later became Hummel Park.

One More Ride?

In 1926, C. T. Snidow opened an amusement park in the rolling hills of West Virginia. For 40 years, people enjoyed the carnival rides and swimming pool. When Lake Shawnee closed in 1966, the rides were deserted. Some of the park's visitors, however, refused to go home.

The swing ride at Lake Shawnee Amusement Park

Around six people are said to have died during Lake Shawnee's history—and a few are thought to still haunt the park. One of the most famous ghost stories dates back to the early 1950s, when a young girl was riding on a twirling swing ride. A truck delivering soda accidentally backed into the swing's path and killed the girl instantly. The owner of Lake Shawnee, Gaylord White, claimed to have seen her ghost ever since.

The spooky girl has been spotted by another family member as well. Once, when White's father was clearing brush with his tractor, he felt someone leaning on his shoulder. The girl's ghost appeared. She said she wanted his tractor, so he got off and gave it to her. The tractor is still sitting in the field where he stopped working.

On quiet summer nights, other spirits make themselves known. It is rumored that the ghostly voices of children can be heard coming from the abandoned park. Maybe they are waiting for the rides to start again. ᓚᘏᗢ

The Ferris wheel, now overgrown with weeds, also has a ghostly passenger. The figure of a man who some say fell to his death on the ride, has been spotted in one of the cars.

Grave Matters

On a warm summer day, children play hide-and-seek at a popular Philadelphia playground. They scramble to find the best hiding places. Little do they know that beneath their feet is a graveyard!

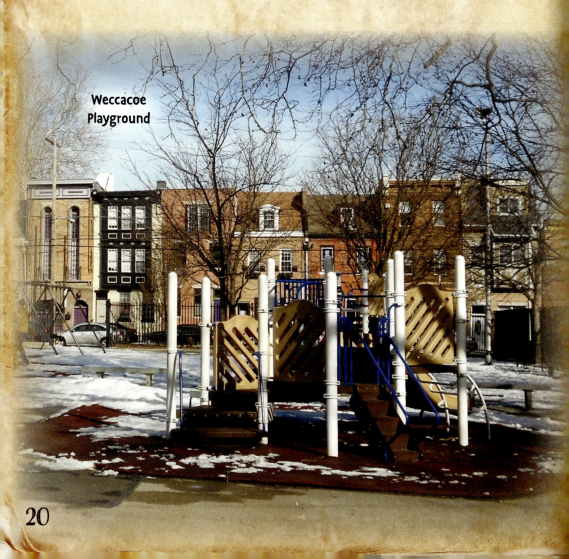

Weccacoe Playground

In the 1800s, there were laws in Philadelphia that kept Black Americans from being buried in the city. Richard Allen, a man who had been freed from slavery, wanted to change that. After he founded a church in the south part of Philadelphia, he bought land for a cemetery for his church members. He called the graveyard Mother Bethel Burial Ground. Over a period of 60 years, more than 5,000 Black Americans were laid to rest there.

By the 1860s, the church had stopped burying people in the cemetery. It became overgrown with weeds and was totally forgotten about. Then in 1889, the city bought the land and turned it into the Weccacoe Playground. In 2013, while the playground was being renovated, the burial ground was rediscovered. Workers uncovered human bones and pieces of broken gravestones. Locals were stunned. One gravestone read: "Whosoever lives and believeth in me, though we be dead, yet shall we live."

In 2018, the city built a memorial in the playground to honor the people buried there.

BETHEL BURYING GROUND

Purchased in 1810 by Mother Bethel A.M.E. Church trustees. It was among the first independent cemeteries for the free Black community. Burials ceased in 1864. The land was sold to the city in 1889. Weccacoe Park was built over the graves of thousands of African Americans.

The word *weccacoe* comes from the language of the Lenape people who were originally of the area. It means peaceful place.

Off the Rails

There were tons of thrills at Old Indiana Fun Park. Visitors could get soaked on the Waterfall log flume. They could also fly down the hills of the Wildcat roller coaster. The miniature train, however, probably didn't seem very exciting. The train chugged through the woods at a calm 12 miles per hour (19 kph). It was a tame ride for little kids—or so most people thought.

The train ride at Old Indiana Fun Park

On August 11, 1996, four-year-old Emily Hunt and her family boarded the miniature train ride at Old Indiana Fun Park. They didn't know that the train had derailed 79 times in the past 2 months. They also were unaware that the safety inspector who cleared the train wasn't licensed to inspect rides. The train frequently went too fast because its speedometer was broken and the train's brakes barely worked—when they worked at all.

As the train approached a curve, two cars leaped off the tracks and flipped over. Emily Hunt broke her neck and was paralyzed for life. Nancy Jones, Emily's grandmother, was thrown from the train. She died when she slammed into a tree. Emily's grandfather broke his leg, her sister broke an arm, and four others in her family were also injured.

The park's owners claimed they didn't know the ride was dangerous. Yet the park closed later that same year, never to open again. Some of the rides were sold. The rest sit rusting in the Indiana sun, a reminder of one girl's horrible pain.

The remains of a swing ride

Emily Hunt's family created a charity for people with spinal cord injuries. To help raise money, they hosted annual walkathons.

23

Creepy in Connecticut

BOOTHE MEMORIAL PARK AND MUSEUM
STRATFORD, CONNECTICUT

For decades, Boothe Park has been the talk of the town. This pretty spot with its quirky buildings is an inviting place for a picnic—and a heart-pounding scare.

Boothe Memorial Park

The Boothe family built a large home in Stratford in the mid-1800s. In the early 1900s, Boothe family members turned the estate into a park—and a shrine to the bizarre.

The property contains a collection of unusual buildings. There's a clock tower, lighthouse, trolley station, chapel, mini-windmill, and an odd building that has no windows or doors. There's also an old cemetery connected to the park. Aside from being an all-around strange place, the cemetery has been the site of many ghostly encounters. The most common is the vision of a hooded figure standing on top of the clock tower. Long-dead Boothe family members have also been spotted on the grounds near the cemetery.

The mini-windmill

One of the most frightening events took place in the cemetery in the 1990s. A visitor walking among the headstones felt sharp stabbing pains in his back and fell to the ground. He later found out that the grave he had fallen on belonged to a Boothe family member who had been stabbed to death!

A visitor to Boothe Memorial Park took a photo of one of the empty buildings. When she looked at the photo later, she saw a ghostly face peering back at her from the picture!

Blaze and Burn

When Electric Park opened, its buildings and towers blazed with the brightness of 100,000 lights. When it closed less than 20 years later, it was still ablaze—only this time it was lit up with yellow and orange flames!

Electric Park

On May 19, 1907, a crowd of 53,000 people arrived for the opening of Electric Park. They were excited to take turns on the roller coaster, the giant swing, the Ferris wheel, and the carousel. Beyond the rides, visitors could also enjoy Electric Park's ballroom, ice cream parlor, shooting gallery, alligator farm, and bowling alley. In the evening, a train traveled around the park while colorful fireworks exploded high above the park's lake.

In 1911, a young Walt Disney, who lived only about 15 blocks away, was one of the park's many visitors. Years later, in 1955, he took inspiration from his visits when he built his own amusement park, Disneyland, in California. Like Electric Park, Disneyland had a train that circled the park and fireworks that lit up the night sky.

Unfortunately, Electric Park did not last long. It caught fire in 1925, and most of the park was reduced to ashes. Some claim it was arson. Unable to rebuild, the owners closed the park with a final fireworks display.

The famous news reporter Walter Cronkite was a boy when he saw the fire at Electric Park. Years later, he said, "Our hill overlooked—a half-dozen blocks away—Electric Park. One night after closing, it burned in a spectacular fire. The Ferris wheel seemed to turn as the flames climbed up its sides."

From Good Times to Ghost Town

When Hurricane Katrina hit Louisiana on August 29, 2005, it was devastating. Thousands of homes were destroyed. More than 1,000 people died. Nearly 80 percent of New Orleans was flooded when its levees failed. Some places were damaged so badly that they never recovered—including the local amusement park.

Six Flags after it was flooded

On August 21, 2005, Six Flags was packed with people. They screamed as they swung through the loops of the Jester coaster. They cooled off in the splashes of the giant log flume. They stood in lines that seemed to last forever for the Batman ride. No one knew this day would be the end of the line for the park.

Eight days later, Katrina hit Six Flags. The hurricane caused water from nearby Lake Pontchartrain (PON-chuhr-*trayn*) to flood the park. The entire area was soon covered with water, in some places as high as 7 ft. (2 m). The water had no place to go, so it sat there for an entire month. By the time it was drained, all of the rides were ruined. Since there was no way to fix them, they were left standing.

As the years passed, the surrounding swamps took over the park. Alligators, snakes, and opossums now make the rotted buildings and rusted rides their home. There is talk about turning the area into a mall. But today the broken, abandoned park still serves as a reminder of the hurricane's tremendous power. ᏬᏍ᳁

In 2012, a film crew took over Six Flags. The abandoned amusement park was the perfect spooky setting to film *Percy Jackson: Sea of Monsters*.

A ride at the abandoned park

29

Garden of Good and Evil

Situated on a hillside along the Hudson River, this park has lovely gardens . . . and killer views. It's also said to have once been the hangout of an infamous murderer.

Untermyer Park

Born in 1858, Samuel Untermyer was a wealthy and respected lawyer. He lived in a grand estate, where he built one of the finest gardens in the country. It included thousands of flowers and huge fountains. Samuel even designed a living sundial made from different plants.

After Samuel died in 1940, the gardens fell into disrepair. For three decades, the once-beautiful grounds became a tangle of weeds. That's when locals began hearing strange chanting coming from the area. Soon, police started finding dead, skinned animals in and around the park. They believed a cult was visiting the property at night. It's said that one of the cult members was David Berkowitz, also known as the Son of Sam. He was sent to prison in 1978 for murdering six people.

Today, the park is once again a beautiful place. However, some people believe that the cult members return when the moon is full.

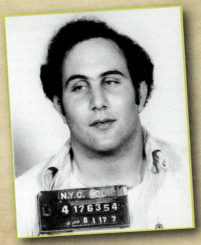

The police photo of David Berkowitz

Every Tuesday, Samuel Untermyer opened his garden to the public. Once, in 1939, more than 30,000 people came to visit!

Eerie Erie Beach

In 1885, Snake Hill Grove was a simple picnic area. By 1928, it had become a million-dollar amusement park known as Erie Beach. Each day, jam-packed ferries and trains brought crowds to the park. With all these visitors, how could Erie Beach close for good only two short years later?

Erie Beach Amusement Park

In the 1920s, a day at the amusement park was an adventure. People could ride a camel in the morning, take a dip in a huge swimming pool after lunch, and dance under the stars to the music of bands that performed at night. In between, visitors could set their hearts racing on the Wildcat roller coaster, the Old Mill Chute, and the Flying Ponies carousel.

Unfortunately, after the stock market crash in 1929, people were broke. Without money to spend, tourists stopped coming. The park quickly became too expensive to run. The owners closed Erie Beach in 1930, leaving it abandoned.

Some people came to view the remains of the once-fabulous park. As it turned out, there was more to see than old stairs leading nowhere and a crumbling boardwalk. Some visitors claimed to see ghosts. Near the area where the Old Mill Chute once stood, people have spotted a small boy. His ghost lingers where he was said to have fallen out of the ride's boat and drowned decades ago.

Erie Beach Amusement Park is located near Fort Erie, a military base in Canada that is hundreds of years old. During the War of 1812, U.S. troops surprised the Canadians in a deadly battle there. Since that time, some have claimed to see the ghosts of long-dead soldiers wandering around the fort.

Troubled Waters

Golden Gate Park, which covers more than 1,000 acres (400 ha), offers an escape from the city of San Francisco. When the fog rolls in, however, the park transforms. It turns into a place where a grieving ghost roams.

Stow Lake at Golden Gate Park

It was a beautiful day in the early 1900s. According to legend, a young mother went for a walk in Golden Gate Park. She pushed her baby in a stroller around Stow Lake, which sparkled in the sunshine. Suddenly, the woman spotted an old friend. They sat down on a bench to talk. The mother parked the stroller beside her. She excitedly chatted with her friend, and then turned to check on her baby. The stroller was gone! She jumped up and ran around the lake, screaming for her lost child. Then, she plunged into the lake to look for her baby—and was never seen alive again.

Is the story true? No one knows for sure. However, for more than 100 years, people have reported seeing a glowing figure on foggy nights. She's dressed in white and nervously circles the lake. Sometimes, she's seen rising from the center of the lake. She often asks people to help her find her baby. Some believe if you say yes, she'll haunt you forever. ꙅ

In 1906, two young girls reported seeing a baby floating in Golden Gate Park. Was it the mother's long-lost baby? We'll never know. Police never found the baby's body.

The Skunk Ape

The Everglades is a big swamp in southern Florida. Giant snakes slither along the ground. Huge alligators lurk in the murky water. And some people say they have seen a creature that's even more terrifying than all the rest!

Everglades National Park

Dave Shealy was 10 years old when he first saw a skunk ape in 1974. "It was walking across the swamp," he later described. "It looked like a man but was completely covered with hair." Shealy was unable to believe his own eyes. According to him, the Bigfoot-like creatures can be up to 7 ft. (2 m) tall and weigh as much as 450 pounds (200 kg). They are covered in shaggy red or black hair and walk on two legs. Skunk apes earned their name because of their horrible smell. People have compared the stink to that of rotting garbage or the smell of dead animals baking in the sun.

Shealy says that skunk apes eat mostly berries, baby birds, and other small animals. However, they have been known to kill large wild boars—and who knows what else. Shealy invites people to come and see for themselves what mysterious creatures are lurking in the Everglades. If you smell something rotten, it might be a skunk ape!

Dave Shealy has studied skunk apes for his entire life. He says the creatures love lima beans and the taste of deer liver!

A skunk ape is a kind of cryptid, an animal whose existence has not yet been proven.

Dead Children's Playground

DROST PARK, HUNTSVILLE, ALABAMA

If you take a walk in Alabama's Maple Hill Cemetery, you might stumble upon something very unusual. There's a playground right next to the graves! It's no surprise that locals call it Dead Children's Playground.

Drost Park, also known as Dead Children's Playground

Maple Hill Cemetery is the largest and oldest cemetery in Alabama. It was founded in 1822 and covers more than 100 acres (40 ha) of land. In 1918, during a flu outbreak, many children died and were buried there. Today, it contains 80,000 bodies. Curiously, the city of Huntsville decided to build a park and playground right next to the cemetery.

Tall, rocky cliffs surround the playground on three sides. It's tucked under a group of large trees, so it's almost always dark and gloomy. At night, however, the place goes from gloomy to ghostly. For years, people have spotted blurry figures playing on the swing set and jungle gym. Eyes are seen glowing in the cliffs. Dust sometimes rises from the footsteps of unseen children. Most curious of all, some say orbs of light float around at what appears to be the same height as young kids. Do the spirits belong to children who were buried in the cemetery?

Maple Hill Cemetery

Legend says that during the 1960s, many children were kidnapped in and around Huntsville. The bodies of some of the children were discovered near where the playground now sits.

The Comet of Death

The jewel of Lincoln Amusement Park was the Comet. For decades, this 3,000-foot- (900-m-) long long wooden roller coaster was the reason many people came there. Yet in the park's final years, the old coaster was the reason some stayed away.

The Comet

In the 1940s, people who were brave enough to board a car on the Comet quickly climbed up 65 ft. (20 m) before the ride went downhill and hit a top speed of 55 mph (85 kph). After 2 minutes and 10 seconds of hills and thrills, the ride was over. Many passengers were scared while riding the wooden roller coaster—but not as frightened as they would come to be in the years ahead.

One of the ride's scariest accidents took place in 1968, when the Comet's last car detached from the rest of the train, rolled backwards, and derailed. The six passengers inside were tossed 10 ft. (3 m) to the ground. In September 1987, faulty brakes caused the last car to once again derail. It hung off the track while its terrified passengers were trapped inside. Following the disaster, many customers stayed away from the dangerous park. It was forced to close less than three months later. ✍

The abandoned Comet before it was torn down

The Comet still stood with the last car hanging from its tracks after the park was closed. Over the years, people sneaked into the park and set parts of it on fire. What was left of the Comet was finally torn down in 2012.

A World of . . .

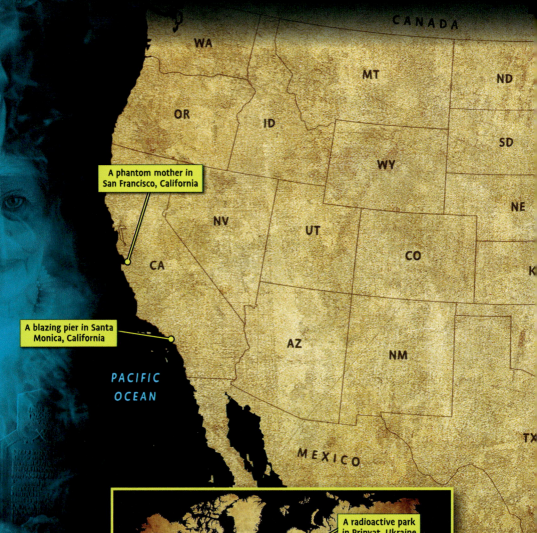

CANADA

WA

MT

ND

OR

ID

SD

WY

NE

NV

UT

CO

K

CA

AZ

NM

A phantom mother in San Francisco, California

A blazing pier in Santa Monica, California

PACIFIC OCEAN

MEXICO

TX

NORTH AMERICA

EUROPE

ASIA

AFRICA

A radioactive park in Pripyat, Ukraine

The night marchers of the Big Island, Hawaii

SOUTH AMERICA

AUSTRALIA

An empty swing in Firmat, Argentina

Petrifying Playtime

A chanting cult in Yonkers, New York

A deadly roller coaster in Dartmouth, Massachusetts

A drowned boy in Ontario, Canada

The Big Dipper Crash in Omaha, Nebraska

The Morphing Stairs in Omaha, Nebraska

A hooded figure in Stratford, Connecticut

A hidden graveyard in Philadelphia, Pennsylvania

A derailed train ride in Thorntown, Indiana

Ghostly children in Mercer County, West Virginia

A fiery Ferris wheel in Kansas City, Missouri

Playground poltergeists in Huntsville, Alabama

A destroyed park in New Orleans, Louisiana

The Skunk Ape in Everglades National Park, Florida

CANADA

MN
WI
MI
IA
IN
IL
OH
MO
KY
AR
TN
NC
MS
AL
GA
SC
LA
FL

ME
VT
NH
NY
MA
CT
RI
NJ
PA
MD
DE
WV
VA

ATLANTIC OCEAN

N
W   E
S

Glossary

abandoned left empty and no longer being used

arson the crime of purposely setting a fire

derailed ran off the tracks

disrepair poor condition due to neglect

evacuated when people are moved away from an area because of danger

ferries boats that carry people, cars, or supplies back and forth between one place and another

gondola a car that travels along a cable high above the ground

grieving feeling very sad after a loss

guardrail a rail that is used for protection, such as one along the side of a highway or roller coaster track

hermit a person who lives alone away from others

hurricane a storm that forms over the ocean, with heavy rains and fast winds of at least 74 mph (119 kph)

infamous well-known for something very bad

infested overrun with lots of insects or animals that can cause harm

inmate someone who has been sent to prison

investigate to search for information about something

lava hot, liquid rock that comes out of a volcano

legend a story from the past that's often not entirely true

levees high walls of dirt and rocks built alongside a body of water to stop flooding

licensed having legal permission to do something

memorial something built to honor or remember people or events

momentum the continued force or speed of movement

morphing changing slowly from one thing to another

native born in or with family from a particular place

nuclear having to do with a type of energy that is produced by splitting atoms

orbs glowing spheres

paralyzed unable to move parts of one's body

penny arcade a building with rows of coin-operated games

pier a structure built over water that is used as a walkway or a landing place for boats

pilings long columns driven into the ground that are used to hold up a pier

plunged entered into suddenly

radiation a form of energy that can be very dangerous when not properly controlled

reactors machines in which a substance called uranium is split to produce nuclear energy

renovated improved the condition of something

residents people who live in a particular place

rubble broken pieces of rock, brick, concrete, and other building materials

safety inspector someone who checks or examines things to make sure they work properly and will not harm anyone

shrine a building associated with holiness

shroud a cloth in which a dead person is wrapped for burial

spinal cord nerve tissue that runs down a person's back and carries messages from the brain to nerves in the body

stock market crash an event in late October 1929 when stocks and bonds suddenly lost value, causing many people to lose their savings

stumped unable to work out what to do or say

sundial an instrument that tells the time of day by using shadows

volcanic formed by a volcano, a kind of mountain that shoots out melted rock and ash

Read More

Hamilton, Sue L. *The World's Most Ghoulish Ghosts (Xtreme Screams)*. Minneapolis: A&D Xtreme, 2022.

Hansen, Grace. *History's Spookiest Paranormal Events (History's Greatest Mysteries)*. Minneapolis: ABDO, 2023.

Marcovitz, Hal. *Teen Guide to the Supernatural*. San Diego, CA: ReferencePoint Press, Inc., 2024.

Williams, Dinah. *True Hauntings: Deadly Disasters*. New York: Scholastic Press, 2020.

Learn More Online

1. Go to **www.factsurfer.com** or scan the QR code below.

2. Enter "**Petrifying Playtime**" into the search box.

3. Click on the cover of this book to see a list of websites.

Index

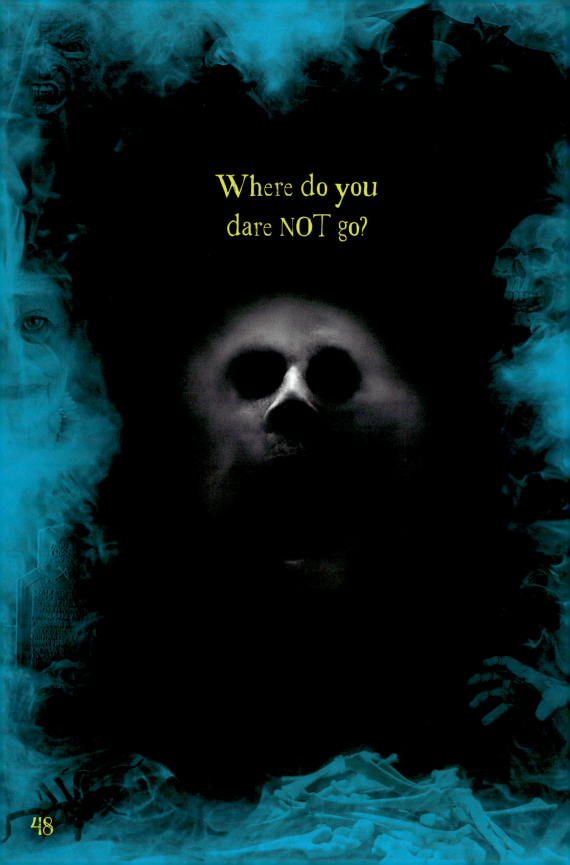

Where do you
dare NOT go?

48